IMAGES
of America

MILWAUKEE COUNTY
PARKS

The *1902 Annual Report of the Park Commissioners of the City of Milwaukee* stated that "golf is altogether the best open-air game ever devised by man, as all sorts of conditions of people can play it; for it suits the physical ability of everybody. It is played in places where the air is pure; it gives incentive for long walks, and that it is doing a vast good for thousands in this city can no longer be questioned." Depicted here are golfers at Lincoln Park where the course opened in 1916.

On the cover: Excavation for the seven-acre lake at West (Washington) Park took place during the summer of 1894 and was completed in November. Boating on the lake was enjoyed by thousands during the following summer. (Courtesy of Milwaukee County Parks.)

IMAGES
of America

MILWAUKEE COUNTY
PARKS

Laurie Muench Albano

ARCADIA
PUBLISHING

Published by Arcadia Publishing
Charleston, South Carolina

Printed in the United States of America

Library of Congress Catalog Card Number: 2007927749

For all general information contact Arcadia Publishing at:
Telephone 843-853-2070
Fax 843-853-0044
E-mail sales@arcadiapublishing.com
For customer service and orders:
Toll-Free 1-888-313-2665

Visit us on the Internet at www.arcadiapublishing.com

*To the citizens of Milwaukee County to whom these parks belong,
and to all those who spent their careers building, maintaining,
and preserving the parks.*

CONTENTS

ACKNOWLEDGMENTS

The author would like to express her gratitude to those who have recorded and preserved the past at the Milwaukee County Parks in the various files and archives—especially my former coworkers Len Engelhardt and Paul Hathaway. Thank you to Lynn Burke for making materials in her care available and to Marie Kerzner for her assistance. The Milwaukee County Historical Society has a load of fun files for use by the public as well as photographs that were copied for this book. Thank you also to the Wisconsin Historical Society for use of the Lueddemann's on the Lake photograph. And, of course, many thanks to my family and friends for their patience and encouragement.

FOREWORD

In 2007, as we observe the 100th anniversary of the founding of the Milwaukee County Park System, this photographic history celebrates that past. It tells the story of how the park system has grown and evolved into what we have today.

This growth and evolution did not just happen. The parks are here by design—through the hard work and vision of civic-minded individuals who wanted Milwaukee to be a great place to live and raise a family.

The result is a 15,000-acre park system that is essentially the backyard for all Milwaukee County citizens. We collectively have ownership of miles of parkway drives, recreational trails and nature trails, tennis courts, baseball diamonds, soccer fields, pools, beaches, pavilions, and dog parks, to name a few. In addition to the many recreational opportunities offered, the parks contribute to our quality of life and protection of our natural resources.

As director of the Milwaukee County Parks, I page through this book and I am humbled by the accomplishments of those who came before me, proud to be a part of this great park system, and energized to move forward and continue to build this important legacy for the future.

Sue Black
Milwaukee County Parks Director

Milwaukee County has an excellent park system, and as county executive I am committed to protecting and enhancing our "Emerald Necklace." Enjoy this book, and I encourage you to get out and explore our parks with your friends and family as much as I do.

Scott Walker
Milwaukee County Executive

One of the area's first white settlers and Milwaukee's first mayor, Solomon Juneau, was immortalized in the garb of his earlier trade—that of a French Canadian fur trader. This statue, located in Juneau Park, was the gift of shoe manufacturers Charles T. Bradley and William H. Metcalf. Juneau's granddaughter Hattie White unveiled the statue on July 6, 1887. Artist Richard Henry Park created the sculpture.

One

PARKS IN EARLY MILWAUKEE

Parks are not a recent development in Milwaukee. They have been a feature of the community since the first settlements were developed here in 1835. The town plats laid out by Solomon Juneau, Byron Kilbourn, George Walker, and their associates contained provision for "public squares" in all three of the communities that formed the early city. Reflecting the traditions of Europe and New England, these areas were included, in part, to offer early residents the opportunity to enjoy green space, relaxation, and fresh air while serving as sites for public gatherings. More often than not, the designation of these open spaces reflected economic or political objectives as much as they did a concern for public health and recreation.

Between 1870 and 1900, Milwaukee's population quadrupled from 70,000 to 285,000. During this period, urban residents were seeking opportunities for recreation. The city had few public sites set aside for park purposes. To meet the needs, numerous private parks or "pleasure gardens" were established. These gardens catered to families and groups who paid a fee to enjoy a combination of entertainment, amusement, and refreshments in addition to fresh air and flowers.

Although the private park era came to an end for a variety of reasons, one of their long-range contributions was to make available land mostly within what had become, by the 20th century, the more developed residential areas of the city. A surprisingly large number of the park sites in the current park system were originally all, or in part, the locations of the 19th-century private parks.

The early plats of Juneautown and Kilbourntown both set aside land for the location of a courthouse. When Juneau and the residents of the east side proved the victors in the struggle for the county seat, the half-block south of the county courthouse became known as Courthouse Square. The original property survives today as Cathedral Square Park.

Scattered throughout the city were small parcels of open land that were oddly shaped through the process of street development. Fourth Ward Square was donated in 1835 by Byron Kilbourn, Solomon Juneau, Albert Fowler, James McCarty, and Archibald Clybourn, pioneers of Milwaukee. "Their gift of this breathing spot stands as a monument to their foresight and civic pride." Today this downtown park is known as Zeidler Union Square.

What is known of today as Burns Commons was originally the First Ward Triangle. The park was a gift of early Milwaukee settler and real estate developer James H. Rogers in 1847. Early development included walks, benches, trees and flower plantings, and a large fountain, which made the park a pleasant gathering place for the nursemaids in this affluent area. The spot was popularly known as "Baby Park." The statue of Scottish poet Robert Burns was added to the park in 1909. James Anderson Bryden, a Scottish immigrant, donated the sculpture. The park came to be known as Robert Burns Triangle, but the name was not officially changed until a city deed restriction was lifted in 1994. The name was more recently modified to Burns Commons.

Walker Square is a 2.1-acre park located between South Ninth and South Tenth Streets from West Mineral to West Washington Streets. The park was originally donated to the city by Col. George Walker in 1836. Walker was an early settler south of the Milwaukee River. He came to the area in 1834 and established a trading post at what became known as Walker's Point. He was mayor of Milwaukee from 1850 to 1851 and again from 1852 to 1853. The Comfort Station in the picture below was added to the park in 1920.

The 2.1 acres of land that make up Clarke Square were donated in 1837 by Nathaniel Brown and Norman and Lydia Clarke, who at the time were real estate developers in that area. The site was officially named Clarke Square in 1890. Initial development, which included planting trees and shrubs, walkway construction, and an ornamental fountain, took place in the early 1900s.

The flushing tunnel site was originally landscaped by the Milwaukee Water Department. Use by the public was secondary to its main purpose of sanitation. This park would eventually be turned over to the city park board as part of the development of the lakefront.

Another facility under the jurisdiction of the water department was the North Point Water Tower. The ornate tower sat on a parklike parcel at North Avenue and Lake Drive. It was one of the principal works in the original water supply system and sat above the water intake station. Often praised for its beauty, the structure was designed in 1873 by architect Charles A. Gombert.

An early city park on the east side of the city overlooking the lakefront was Juneau Park. It was originally under the jurisdiction of the public works department. The original park was a narrow strip of land along the bluff above the railroad tracks. The Chicago and Northwestern railway depot can be seen in the distance of this 1913 photograph. Designed by architect Charles S. Frost, the structure became a commanding presence on the lakefront when it was built in 1889. Its 234-foot tower could be seen from well over 20 miles out into the lake.

Juneau Place, as it was called at the time, was one of the only public spots along the lakefront where early Milwaukeeans could sit and enjoy the picturesque views of the lake. Juneau Park is now a tree-filled 15 acres along the top of the bluff overlooking Lake Michigan between Juneau Avenue on the north and Mason Street to the south.

This early view looking north along the lake from Juneau Park shows a less handsome picture. The railroad tracks prevented easy access to the lake's edge. It took a tremendous amount of vision to turn this eyesore into the lakefront that is the pride of Milwaukee today.

If one thinks festivals at the lakefront are a new phenomenon, one probably has not heard of the annual Court of Neptune Pageant held on this "island" east of Juneau Park. This photograph shows crowds at the 1926 pageant, which ran August 6 through August 8.

Pabst Park 1902

The private gardens or parks of 19th-century Milwaukee were largely the result of the influx of European immigrants beginning in the 1840s. The European tradition of the neighborhood "bier gartens," brought to Milwaukee by pre–Civil War German immigration, emphasized the opportunities for social contact and entertainment in an outdoor setting. Capt. Frederick Pabst bought the site of the former *schuetzen*, or shooting park (home of the Milwaukee Schuetzen Gesellschaft, or shooting club), that was located between North Third and North Fifth Streets south of West Burleigh Street and made it a popular amusement park. It featured a figure eight roller coaster that was 15,000 feet long. Today the site is home of the Clinton Rose Senior Center and Rose Park.

Quentin's Park near Walnut and North Eighth Streets was acquired by the Joseph Schlitz Brewing Company in 1879 and became one of the most popular beer gardens in the city in the 1880s and 1890s. In the center of the park was a hill topped by a three-story pavilion from which most of the city could be seen. Part of this site is today's Carver Park. (Courtesy of the Milwaukee County Historical Society.)

In addition to their role in providing outdoor recreation for Milwaukee residents, these private parks also served community organizations, churches, and schools in a similar manner. Lueddemann's Farm, also known as Lueddemann's on the Lake, had a large clientele on Sunday afternoons; the people walked or came by wagon from Milwaukee, which was two hours away by foot. The farm was one of the first tracts purchased by the city in 1890 for Lake Park. (Courtesy of Wisconsin Historical Society, image No. Whi-28085.)

Two

A CITY PARK BOARD IS ESTABLISHED

Toward the end of the 19th century, the city of Milwaukee was faced with the need to improve public services for its rapidly growing urban population. It was at this time that the Milwaukee Board of Park Commissioners was created. The first park board was appointed by Mayor Thomas H. Brown. It was composed of five members—civic and business leaders who served without pay. They were Christian Wahl, president; Calvin E. Lewis; Charles Manegold Jr.; Louis Auer; and John Bentley.

In 1889, the state legislature passed laws allowing the City of Milwaukee and its park commission to purchase land with money raised from the sale of bonds. The new park board first assembled in June 1889, and its first order of business was to locate appropriate sites to purchase for parks. The commissioners personally inspected every available tract of land within city limits, "keeping in view the fundamental idea that such tracts should be chosen which offered the best natural advantages, and which were so located as to afford accommodations for the greatest possible number and still adhere to the general scheme of having a chain of parks around the city connected by handsome boulevards." By October 1890, they had agreed upon five sites to purchase. These sites became Lake Park, Riverside Park, Mitchell Park, Kosciuszko Park, and Humboldt Park.

As the city boundaries expanded, the park board soon found the original legislation too restrictive. New legislation in 1891 allowed the board to purchase land anywhere in Milwaukee County where desirable sites and reasonable prices were more readily available. Land was then purchased for Washington and Sherman Parks.

With these early land purchases, the board had gone over $800,000 in debt, so no new lands were purchased for the next 16 years. Additionally, the city park system grew much more rapidly than the revenue provided for in order to maintain it. When new buildings were erected (payment for which was generally made by bond issue) or new park features were added, additional commensurate revenues were not provided. Financial problems became a constant obstacle to the growth of the city park system. Despite this, however, their accomplishments were nothing short of amazing.

Christian Wahl was a wealthy businessman who served as president of the park commission from 1889 to 1899. Born in 1829 in Bavaria, Wahl immigrated with his parents to Milwaukee in 1846. He spent his career in Chicago where he also served on the city council and the board of education. Upon retirement, Wahl returned to Milwaukee to reside in a home on Prospect Avenue. (Courtesy of the Milwaukee County Historical Society.)

An excerpt from the *1892 Annual Report of the Park Commission* states that, "Realizing the large parks would require the services of experts in the line of landscape architecture, the commissioners decided to engage the best talent obtainable, and accordingly entered into negotiations with the firm of Frederick Law Olmsted & Co. of Brookline, Massachusetts." Olmsted's firm eventually provided the basic layout for Lake Park, Riverside Park, and Washington Park.

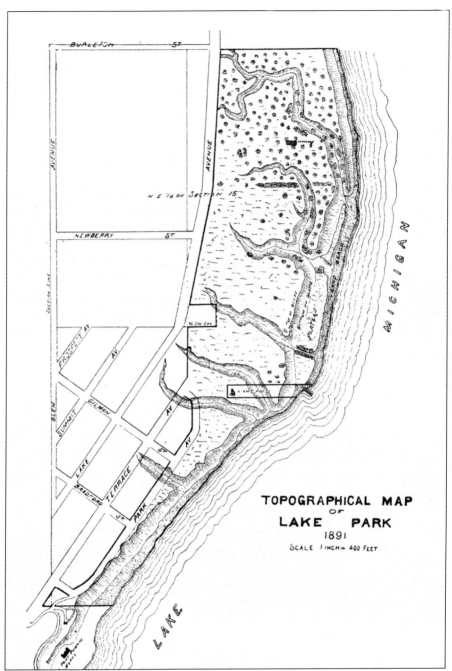

TOPOGRAPHICAL MAP
OF
LAKE PARK
1891
SCALE 1 INCH = 400 FEET

One of the first purchases made for the new park system was 123.6 acres located along the Lake Michigan shoreline, extending from the Water Works Park at Terrace Avenue north to Burleigh Street. The property was cut by several ravines, which extended to the lake. The northern 40 acres of the park were heavily wooded, consisting primarily of oaks. The commissioners saw this as the only chance left to provide the citizens of Milwaukee with an opportunity to reach the lake without having to cross railroad tracks as "private landholders and corporations had ownership of the lakeshore from St. Francis on the south to the Water Works on the north."

Originally built in 1855 of cream city brick, the North Point Light Station is depicted here in 1890. The tower was 28 feet tall and was situated on a bluff that made it, at 107 feet above the water, the highest lighthouse elevation on the Great Lakes. Several decades of erosion brought the light station perilously close to the bluff edge, and the U.S. Lighthouse Service made a decision to rebuild it 100 feet west in 1888.

Frederick Law Olmsted's plan for the park contemplated a grand carriage drive between the lakeshore and the new lighthouse, taking advantage of the vista along the lakefront. The commissioners successfully negotiated with the federal government and were allowed to improve the lighthouse parcel, which essentially cut the park in half. In 1897, two steel arch bridges spanning the ravines north and south of the lighthouse were completed and adorned with eight sculpted stone lions.

An iron and steel footbridge, designed by local bridge engineer Oscar Sanne, was built across the North Ravine in 1892. The bridge was 110 feet long and 12 feet wide. The terra-cotta railing on the abutments was completed in 1893.

This rustic footbridge was built across the South Ravine in 1895. It was planned by park board president Christian Wahl. Additional rustic bridges were built across the brooks in the bottom of the ravines under Wahl's direction, providing pedestrian access down to the lakefront.

A railcar station, with a large waiting room and "retiring rooms," was built in 1894 from plans made by architect Howland Russel. The structure was located at the Folsum (Locust) Street entrance, which allowed visitors to easily visit the park using "the electric road." This station cost about $7,000, one half of which was paid by the Milwaukee Street Railway Company.

A pavilion and a bandstand were built in Lake Park and opened to the public in 1903. The pavilion was described as having a floor space of 140 feet by 50 feet with two porches that measured 26 feet by 26 feet at the west end. The basement was outfitted with all sanitary conveniences.

Lake Park, Wahl Monument, 19

A monument erected to the memory of the late Christian Wahl by the citizens of Milwaukee was placed immediately in front of the Lake Park pavilion and unveiled on July 11, 1903. The bust was relocated to a new neighborhood park located at North Forty-eighth Street and Hampton Avenue that was named in Wahl's honor in 1956.

On the east side of the pavilion was a "grand stair" that provided access to the lakefront. The original layout included a stadium where crowds gathered to watch sporting events and military reviews in the early 1900s. The stadium was eventually removed to make way for the lakeshore drive.

According to early park commission records, "The afternoon concerts at Lake Park, coupled with the excellent transportation facilities [of the new railcar station], drew great crowds to this shady and cool lake plateau, there being thousands of people in this park several Sundays during the summer."

A six-hole golf link was laid out in Lake Park in the spring of 1903 and was "well patronized during the summer months." The park was heavily used on weekends and holidays. Picnickers and those who came to stroll did not hesitate to cross anywhere in the portion of the park that had been set aside for golf and caused considerable friction between park patrons.

A tool and wagon shed was built north of Burleigh Street (now Kenwood Boulevard) and was completed in 1899. The building was to serve a number of purposes, such as a wagon shed, carpenter shop, blacksmith shop, office, and storage room for tools and other park implements. The structure was enlarged and remodeled in 1918.

Dr. Erastus B. Wolcott was surgeon general of Wisconsin during the Civil War years and made surgical history in 1861 as the first physician to remove a diseased kidney. This equestrian statue by sculptor Francis Herman Packer was dedicated on June 12, 1920. It was financed by the estate of Wolcott's widow, Dr. Laura Ross Wolcott, and is located in Lake Park east of the golf course.

A very important component of the park commissioners' overall plan was to create landscaped boulevards connecting the parks. Newberry Boulevard, shown here, ran from the entrance of Lake Park on the east to Riverside Park on the west. A map showing a system of parks and boulevards for the general plan of the city was completed in 1891.

This cast bronze sculpture was donated to the park commission in 1928 by neighbors of Lake Park and placed in an ornamental fountain north of Locust Street. Sculptor Girolamo Piccoli, who at the time was chair of the modeling department at Layton School of Design, created *Boy with Goose*. According to a newspaper account, the real-life model for the figure was Dominic Joseph Balistrieri, who later became a city of Milwaukee fireman who died in 1961. Piccoli was born in Palermo, Sicily, in 1902. He came to Milwaukee at the age of four and grew up here.

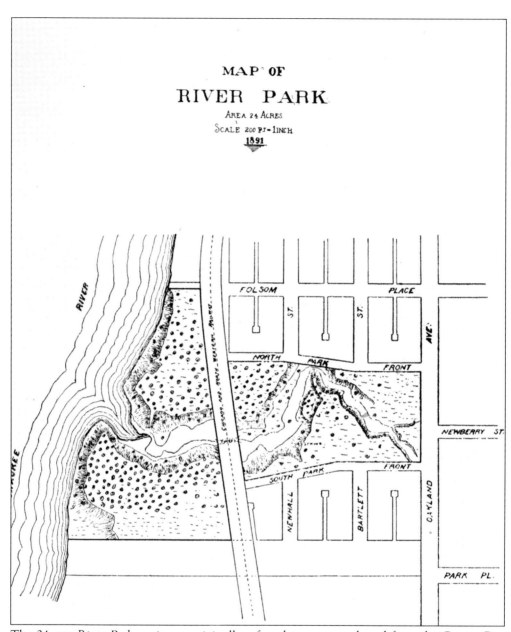

MAP OF

RIVER PARK.

AREA 24 ACRES

SCALE 200 FT = 1INCH

1891

The 24-acre River Park, as it was originally referred to, was purchased from the Cream City Land Company in 1890. The park commissioners described it as "a picturesque little tract cuddled down in the valley of the Milwaukee River above the dam, its location such that ample opportunities for boating in the summer and skating in the winter are afforded." One drawback to the property was that it was bisected by the Chicago and Northwestern Railroad tracks. The commissioners were able to overcome this obstacle by working with the railroad to build a culvert under the tracks "to afford safe passage from one part of the park to the other." The park was officially named Riverside Park by the commissioners in 1900.

The majority of activity at Riverside Park centered around recreation on the river. This 1915 photograph depicts skaters on the Milwaukee River between Riverside and Gordon Parks. A sheet of ice about seven acres in size attracted thousands of people of all ages on evenings and Sunday afternoons throughout the winter.

The large trees on the plateaus above the Milwaukee River provided a shady spot for picnics. During the week days hundreds of schoolchildren, under the care of their teachers, frequented the parks. The picture here is of a Fratney Street School picnic taken on June 12, 1920. The parks were such popular picnic spots that the park commission issued special permits to the teachers—200 were issued in 1901.

Originally known as West Park or the Vliet Street Tract, the land for Washington Park was purchased in 1891. Early development in the park followed the plan developed by F. L. Olmsted and Company. This vista is typical of the pastoral landscape scenes Frederick Law Olmsted was famous for creating, including those in his design of Central Park in New York.

A new lake was constructed in the northeast section of Washington Park in 1907 and connected to the old lake with a 50-foot-wide passage. The new section of the lake was about four acres and was only four and a half feet deep to make it safer in case a boat overturned. This picture, taken in 1914, shows boaters passing under an ornamental concrete bridge that was constructed between old and new sections of the lake.

It was the intent of the commissioners to "make Washington Park the home of all athletic sports," and in the early 1900s, an athletic field and a half-mile track were built. A field house and grandstand were added after 1913. With one side fronting the lagoon, the building was to be used by skaters and boaters as well as for field sports.

The half-mile track was used for horse races after Mayor Sherburn M. Becker sent a request to the park board in 1908. He wrote that the track would be used by "an organization in the city known as Gentlemen's Driving Club composed of a large number of prominent citizens who have associated to encourage the breeding and use of high grade horses of which there are too few in Milwaukee. It has been their practice to have matinee races for prizes but never for money."

This handsome bandstand with a foundation of split boulders was designed by architect Howland Russel and was completed in the early spring of 1896. One of the most popular features in the park was the summer night concerts that took place here.

In 1905, after repeated requests to the common council, the park commission was no longer billed by the city for water used in the parks. The money saved was used to install playgrounds in many of the parks. A children's playground was located south of the concert grove in Washington Park in 1906 and included a cement wading pool and play apparatus.

The Fourth of July was a day full of family fun and festivities such as the doll parade that is depicted here in Washington Park in 1914. The young girls are dressed in their finest outfits as they show off their patriotically decorated doll buggies.

The park police force was established in 1891 and was responsible for maintaining order in the parks. It was charged with "protecting the weak, curbing the vicious, and also acting as custodians of all park properties." Attired in gray uniforms, the force is pictured here in 1914 in front of the original pavilion designed by Howland Russel in 1892.

On July 3, 1921, the Frederick Wilhelm Von Steuben equestrian statue was unveiled at the Sherman Boulevard entrance to Washington Park. Sculpted by J. Otto Schweizer, it was a gift of the Muehlenberg unit of the Von Steuben Society, a German American cultural organization. Von Steuben was recognized for the introduction of infantry drill formations and regulations during the American Revolution to a previously inexperienced Continental army.

This monument to the playwright Johann Wolfgang von Goethe and poet Johann Christoph Friedrich von Schiller was created by sculptor Ernst Rietschel and dedicated on June 14, 1908. Presented by 30 German American cultural societies, the sculpture represents pride in the artistic achievements of the German people. It was moved to a site near the Blatz Temple of Music in order to make way for the construction of U.S. Highway 41. It was rededicated on September 11, 1960.

The Temple of Music band shell in Washington Park was given by brewer Emil Blatz (right). The $100,000 donation was one of the largest ever received by one of Milwaukee's citizens. The first performance in August 1938 was of Gilbert and Sullivan's *The Gondoliers* performed by the International Opera Chorus. The program took place while the "plaster was still wet and the permanent sound system was not yet in place." The band shell was dedicated a week later on August 23, 1938, with popular radio singer Jessica Dragonette performing to a crowd estimated at 40,000 persons. NBC and CBS radio broadcast parts of the concert to the nation. During the next few decades, some of the nation's leading singers and instrumental groups performed there, principally in the Music Under the Stars series. Architect Fitzhugh Scott designed the music temple.

The original plan for Washington Park featured a "deer paddock." In 1892, park commissioner Louis Auer and Col. Gustave Pabst donated seven deer to the city for the west side park. The gift was received by the commissioners with thanks, and the matter was referred to the west side commissioners in order to prepare suitable quarters for the deer. A deer park, enclosing about an acre, was built.

The 1905 annual report stated that it was the intention of the commissioners to annually enlarge and improve the zoo in Washington Park and to eventually make it the equal to any in the country. The sea lion tank shown here was added in 1907 when two sea lions were donated by the citizens of the 22nd Ward. The oval pool featured a rustic stone island in the center with a grotto shelter for the sea lions.

According to the 1906 *Proceedings of the Board of Park Commissioners of the City of Milwaukee,* "Great interest has been shown in the establishment of this zoo by our citizens; great numbers of our citizens have expressed their gratification and have offered to donate specimens, and have also created a so-called 'Milwaukee Zoological Society,' which organization has been duly incorporated and the object of which is to aid the city in enlarging and perfecting the zoological garden in Washington Park. It behooves us to erect the necessary buildings to shelter the animals which the citizens are willing to donate as soon as they know that they can be taken care of."

In 1906, Edward H. Bean (left), an animal keeper from the Lincoln Park Zoo in Chicago, was engaged to care for the growing collection of animals, which, by this time, was up to about 75 in number. He went on to become the first director of the Washington Park Zoo (below). Bean resigned in 1927 to become the director of the Brookfield Zoo in Illinois. The great strides gained by the Washington Park Zoo in its early years have been directly attributed to Bean's competency and leadership.

This beautiful classical entrance to the new animal building at the zoo, constructed to house small mammals, was completed late in 1907. It was designed by Albert C. Clas after a visit to some of the principal zoos in the country with commissioners August Rebhan and Henry Weber. The building would ultimately be the center of a group of three.

A unique addition to the zoological garden in Washington Park and one that attracted great attention was the monkey island. Monkeys housed in various parts of the zoo were put on the island, which opened in the spring of 1921. The inventory of zoo animals for the end of that year lists 52 monkeys of at least 20 different species.

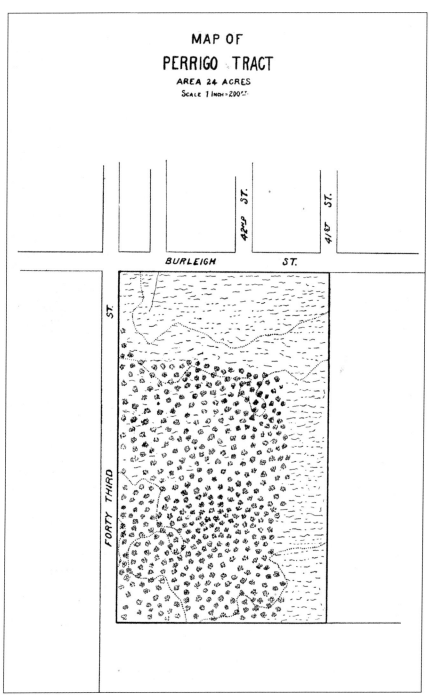

MAP OF
PERRIGO TRACT
AREA 24 ACRES
SCALE 1 INCH = 200'

Sherman Park was originally referred to as North Park or the Perrigo Tract, after the family from which the 24 acres of parkland were purchased in 1891. The property was described in the 1891 annual report (same as page 23) as "a level piece of land more than half of which was covered by fine timber and admirably suited for park purposes." It was located at Forty-third and Burleigh Streets in what was a relatively unsettled part of the city. Early improvements to the park were minor.

A pavilion was constructed in Sherman Park in 1900 to accommodate picnic parties and social gatherings. At the time, it was still a mile walk to the nearest streetcar line. In December 1907, this structure burned to the ground as the city's water supply had not yet reached the vicinity of park. The pavilion was reconstructed in 1908. As the city's population grew, the park was used more heavily. Shown here is a photograph of the annual picnic of McKinley Lodge No. 307 on August 16, 1919.

The Honorable John L. Mitchell (1842–1904), a representative and senator from Wisconsin, sold 25 acres of his south side property to the park board in 1891 and donated an additional six acres. Called "the gem of the south side parks," Mitchell Park was named in his honor. At the time of its purchase in 1891, it was described as "a high piece of rolling ground, overlooking the Menomonee Valley and studded with many old trees in a fine state of preservation." (Courtesy of the Milwaukee County Historical Society.)

Boating at Mitchell Park
August 2-1914

A lake was excavated in a natural basin in Mitchell Park in 1891, and a rustic-style structure was built to be used as a boathouse in the summer and as a shelter for skaters in the winter. In 1892, the park board reported the great success of renting rowboats on the lake at Mitchell Park, stating, "This was in every respect a complete success and was the means of affording recreation to hundreds of children and not a few grown people during the summer and fall."

In 1898, the most important work in the way of improvements in Mitchell Park was the beginning of the new conservatory. The park board exclaimed, "When completed this building will provide a beautiful winter garden during the time that our rigid climate will forbid the visiting of our other parks. It will not only in itself be a great ornament to the park." The plans for the conservatory were drawn by Milwaukee architects C. Koch and Company.

The beautiful wrought iron gates in this entrance to the conservatory were created by Austrian-born metal craftsman Cyril Colnik (1871–1957). Often referred to as "the Tiffany of wrought iron masters," it was popular to have his ironwork as part of the architectural elements of affluent homes and institutions. He was so highly regarded for his sense of style that architects noted on their blueprints, "Colnik to design ironwork."

Chrysanthemum display, Mitchel Park

Greenhouses adjacent to the conservatory were used to grow thousands of plants for the parks and boulevards as well as for the seasonal displays in the new conservatory. The colorful mum show depicted here was a popular place to visit as cool fall weather set in.

The sunken garden in Mitchell Park was added in 1903. The 1904 park commission annual report claims that, "Anyone seeing this formal garden and its surroundings in its summer garb would not imagine that no more than three years ago this was a truck farmer's garden." It also stated that, "The event of the season was the midsummer night festival, when the formal garden and fountains were illuminated by thousands of Chinese lanterns, and visitors had the pleasure of viewing the work of the season and listening to the beautiful music of Bach's orchestra."

Humboldt Park, originally referred to as Howell Avenue Park and South Park, was an undulating tract of land with 30 of its 45 acres covered by fine timber. Early work in the park included the construction of a lake. A handsome boathouse, designed by architect Howland Russel, was built on the south shore of the lake in 1892.

Bay View's memorial to its 1,200 World War I veterans was dedicated in Humboldt Park on May 22, 1921. A military and civil parade preceded the dedication. The monument was made by the American Granite Company and paid for by popular subscription. The sculpture is located in the southeast corner of the park on a rise north of the lily pond.

Humboldt Park 1895
J. BROWN. PHOTO.
85. P.

One of the most popular features of Humboldt Park has always been the lily pond. Constructed in 1892, the park commissioners boasted, "The great attraction of the year was the lily pond at 'South Park.' The blooming of the mammoth lily, the Amazon, the Victoria regia, took thousands of people out to this handsome little park who had not hitherto dreamed of the existence of this beauty spot on the south side."

Kosciuszko Park is another of the original park commission purchases made in 1890. It started out as a 26-acre tract with an addition of almost 11 acres in 1902. Situated in a heavily populated area of the city, it was always well patronized. It was referred to as the Coleman Tract and Lincoln Avenue Park until it was officially named Kosciuszko Park in 1900 upon the request of "the Polish citizens of the area."

Skating was a popular activity on the lagoons in all of the south side parks. Excavation for the Kosciuszko lagoon began in 1892 and was further expanded in 1904. The boathouse was originally built on the east shore of the lake. It was moved to the north shore of the expanded lake in 1905.

An 1893 park commission report described progress in Kosciuszko Park as, "the park having been brought into such condition as to be thoroughly enjoyed by picnic parties. A drinking fountain for horses was erected in the center of the concourse and one for visitors to the park, at the intersection of two walks near the pavilion." In 1918, the park was home to this celebration of the first anniversary of the formation of the Polish army in France.

Gen. Thaddeus Kosciuszko served as military engineer to Gen. George Washington during the Revolutionary War and later designed the fortification at West Point. This statue, located in Kosciuszko Park, which was named for him, was sculpted by Gaetano Trentanove. It was the gift of the Polish National Alliance and was dedicated on June 18, 1905. In 1951, the monument was relocated to face Lincoln Avenue and rededicated on September 16 of that year.

This statue of a young girl feeding a squirrel was erected in honor of Belle Austin Jacobs, the founder of the University Settlement Club. For 27 years, Jacobs was co-warden of the club and was considered a pioneer social worker among the Polish people in Milwaukee. The artist creating this work was Sylvia Shaw Hudson of Chicago. This beautiful memorial was stolen from Kosciuszko Park on December 16, 1975, and was never recovered.

In 1907, the park board was authorized by the common council to advertise for bids for a tract of land containing approximately 150 acres to be used for park purposes and to be situated north of the city. The commissioners were most impressed with an offer of 159 acres known as Lindwurm Farm. They felt it was ideally located with Green Bay Road on the west, Hampton Avenue on the north, and Port Washington Road on the east.

Early improvements in the park included a roadway leading from Green Bay Road across the Milwaukee River to Port Washington Road. This concrete arch bridge was constructed between 1913 and 1914. Also at this time the name of the park was changed from Lindwurm Park to Lincoln Park.

Gordon Park was acquired in 1907 and was located directly across the Milwaukee River from Riverside Park. During the early 1900s, these two parks were centers for river-related activities. Warm weather found the river devoted to boating and swimming. The Gordon Park pavilion, depicted here, was built in 1914.

In the winter months, a toboggan slide in Riverside Park provided thrills by crossing a giant hump constructed on the river's ice and ending up in Gordon Park. A ski jump in Gordon Park provided a venue for competitions, and the frozen riverbed between the parks was the scene of winter carnivals that drew huge crowds to events such as hockey games and skating races.

In late 1907, the park commissioners purchased an 80-acre parcel once known as Reynold's Grove, which had been a popular private park on the south side. Later named Jackson Park, the site became a favorite picnic spot for families and school and church groups. On July 24, 1921, the Trinity Evangelical Lutheran Church began its picnic with a service in the park.

The Statue of Commerce was dedicated on June 26, 1909, in Jackson Park and was the gift of the South Division Civic Association. The statue had been given to the association by Theobald Otjen, president of the Central Investment Company, who owned the chamber of commerce building. The statue, created by sculptor Gustav Haug, had formerly stood over the entrance to the building.

Early on, the commissioners realized the importance of preserving the lakefront for public purposes. They found that most of the property was already privately owned and could not be secured except at a prohibitive cost. Therefore, it was planned to reclaim a strip of submerged land along the shoreline, and for this purpose, two grants were secured from the state and federal government in 1893 and 1897.

This elegant concrete bridge, designed by architects George B. Ferry and Albert C. Clas, was completed in 1905. The following year, a drive was built that started at the head of the north ravine in Lake Park, continued under the bridge, and extended for 1,000 feet along the lakeshore. The beach drive ended in a concourse and a hitching place for horses opposite the government lighthouse.

Because of the lack of funds, the park board was unable to do much more work on extending the lakeshore drive until 1907 when the legislature authorized the expenditure of a fixed percentage of the tax levy for the project. The work started in earnest in 1908 when a revetment was constructed from the Milwaukee River flushing tunnel south to East Wisconsin Avenue.

Filling went on for a number of years, and in 1922, the matter of a bridge across the railroad tracks was discussed with the Chicago and Northwestern Railway Company. A contribution of $130,000 was made by the railroad toward the construction of the Lincoln Memorial Bridge in fulfillment of an agreement that had been made with the city in 1872.

Lake Front Developme
1927

On September 28, 1929, Lincoln Memorial Drive was officially opened for its entire length from downtown Milwaukee to the north end of Lake Park. Almost all of it was on land reclaimed from the lake. The same holds true for parts of Juneau, McKinley, Bradford, and Lake Parks, through which the drive passes. A similar reclamation project on the south side resulted in additional frontage for South Shore Park.

Three

CREATION OF
THE COUNTY
PARK COMMISSION

In the early 1900s, a group of city leaders felt that a broader vision for growth of the surrounding region was needed. Formal creation of the Milwaukee County Park Commission was accomplished by action of the Wisconsin legislature in the spring of 1907 in response to the efforts of a group of concerned Milwaukee area park supporters. Chapter 250, Laws of 1907 not only allowed for the creation of the commission but assigned the new body responsible for making a thorough study of the county to identify lands suitable for public use and to lay out a plan for open areas, roads, and boulevards as part of "a comprehensive plan for a county park system." Reports on this planning were to be submitted to the board of supervisors within two years.

On August 20, 1907, Charles T. Fisher, chairman of the Milwaukee County Board of Supervisors, made the necessary appointments to the commission as called for by the law. The first park commissioners were influential and respected members of the Milwaukee community who, either through their business activities or personal interests, were well qualified to serve.

They set out on their mission planning for the expansion of the county, identifying major travel routes from city center into the outlying areas, proposed lands to be set aside for parks and parkways, and laid out residential neighborhoods adjacent to these lands. The park system would initially focus on securing land for major parks geographically dispersed and connected by parkways along major waterways. Their success is evident in the park system that is enjoyed today.

William Lindsay served on the park commission from 1907 until 1919. He was an operator of a farm implement company, a state assemblyman, and later an alderman. At the first meeting of the Milwaukee County Park Commission in September 1907, Lindsay was elected the commission's first president, an office he held until 1918.

One of the original park commission members, Alfred C. Clas served from 1907 until he resigned in 1917. He also served three terms on the city park board. Clas was trained as an architect and associated himself in business with George B. Ferry. The Milwaukee firm of Ferry and Clas became widely known, receiving gold medal awards for their designs. Clas died in July 1942 at the age of 82.

Patrick Cudahy, one of the original county park commissioners, served until his death in 1919. He founded and promoted the industrial city of Cudahy. Starting out as a meat packer, Cudahy became superintendent of Plankinton and Armour in 1874 and purchased the company in 1888. It then became the Cudahy Company. In 1893, he moved the company to the city of Cudahy.

Emerson Hoyt served on the park commission from 1907 until 1921 and became its second president. Hoyt became one of the incorporators of the village of Wauwatosa and served as its second president. He had the honor of serving as the mayor after the city was incorporated in 1897. He died in 1924 at the age of 77.

Alvin P. Kletzsch was a real estate dealer and operator of the old Republican Hotel that had been built by his father, Charles Frederick Kletzsch. He played football during college in New Jersey and became the University of Wisconsin's first football coach in 1887. He served on the park commission from 1907 until 1941 and was named its vice president in 1935.

James Currie was a founder of Currie Brothers, Seedsmen and Florists and superintendent for many years of Forest Home Cemetery. Currie emigrated from Scotland at the age of 19. He was an original member of the county park commission and served until his death in 1922. Currie was also a member of the city park board for 11 years. (Courtesy of the Milwaukee County Historical Society.)

Charles Whitnall served for 40 years as a park commissioner from 1907 until he resigned on July 1, 1947, and simultaneously served as secretary from 1919 until 1926. He is generally recognized as the father of the county park system. From 1907, and particularly following his selection as secretary in 1919, Whitnall's role in county park affairs was a commanding one. His philosophy dominated the early plans and programs of the commission. Born in 1859, Whitnall became his father's assistant in his florist business at the age of 16 and eventually took over the business. In 1888, he opened the first Wholesale Commission Flower Market in Milwaukee. He also originated the Florist Telegraph Delivery System that made it possible to have flowers delivered in any principal city of the world. From 1910 to 1912, he was city treasurer. Whitnall was known as a strong supporter of the socialist party. He died on January 5, 1949, at the age of 90.

Another important player in the creation of the county park system was Milwaukee attorney Charles E. Estabrook. A power in Civil War veterans' circles, Estabrook was a member of the state legislature, serving as assemblyman for Milwaukee's 13th District. Estabrook was able to guide the necessary enabling legislation that created the county park commission through both houses of the legislature. The bill, emerging as Chapter 250, Laws of 1907, took effect on July 1 of that year. Although never appointed a member of the seven-man commission, Estabrook played a leading role as its secretary for more than a decade until his death in early 1919.

The identification and acquisition of desirable parkland would be a major task for the new county park commissioners but only within the much broader framework of planning for the systematic development of the county outside the city of Milwaukee. As the county expanded, developers touted the benefits of their newly platted subdivisions adjacent to proposed parkways.

An adequate highway network with rules governing setbacks for buildings along main roads was seen as particularly essential to the relationship of residential areas with the outlying parks. The commissioners urged that Grand Avenue be developed as the main road between Milwaukee and the state capital and be named Wisconsin Avenue. This picture was labeled as "Ugly Approach to Grand Avenue Viaduct."

A system of parkways, following routes of major waterways in the county, also provided connecting links between primary park areas. The park commissioners developed a campaign to convince the county board and local citizens of the merits of reserving land along rivers and streams for park use, for the purpose of flood control for nearby residential areas, and to reduce pollution in the waterways. These two photographs were used as examples of good and bad development along the Kinnickinnic and Milwaukee Rivers.

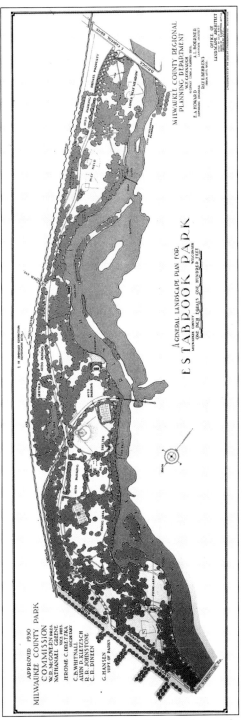

Starting in 1916, substantial portions of Estabrook Park bordering the upper Milwaukee River were obtained, along with the Blatz Farm property (Kletzsch Park) farther north along the river two years later. The park was named for Charles E. Estabrook in 1919 shortly after his death.

The inclusion of a mill tax for parks in the annual county budget substantially increased the ability of the commission to embark on its land acquisition program. The first land purchases in 1910 were Bluff Park, located just north of the Soldiers Home, followed by the initial section of Jacobus Park along the Menomonee River in Wauwatosa, shown here.

The 1911 purchase of 292 acres for Grant Park in South Milwaukee had over a mile of frontage on Lake Michigan. The park commissioners promoted the acquisition, saying, "For the purpose desired this tract of land is fully up to our well known and highly prized Lake Park. Lake Park however, has an area of only 125 acres while the proposed reservation has an area of 292 acres. Lake Park cost $2,164 per acre, while the land desired by your commission can be secured at an estimated cost of not exceeding $350 to $375 per acre."

As the park system grew in size, so did the demand for programs and recreational development. County supervisor Charles Jacobus, a longtime supporter of the park commission, urged his colleagues to go on record supporting a broad recreational program through the creation of facilities for baseball, tennis, golf, and other such athletic activities. There was particular need, he pointed out, for a golf course to be designed and developed at "the South Milwaukee Park." This is an early photograph of the golf course that was developed soon thereafter.

Local golf enthusiasts recommended to the commission that George Hansen, then in charge of a golf course in Racine, be retained to layout and operate the proposed course. He was hired as golf manager in 1919, with a starting salary of $150 per month, plus the privilege of selling golf equipment, candy, and cigars, providing lessons, and repairing clubs. Hansen would go on to be appointed the first park superintendent in 1926, a position he remained in until his death in 1950.

Now known as the Grant Park clubhouse, Horace N. Fowle built this house in 1892 on the exact site of the log cabin in which he was born in 1837. Fowle and his wife, Ellen (Thompson), had nine children and needed the 11-room structure to house their family. In 1907, the Fowle family offered to sell their land on Lake Michigan to the county, but the park commission showed little interest until Patrick Cudahy offered to put up his own money at no interest to the commission.

In 1919, there were several proposals from individual county board members that indicated that they felt the commission was much too concerned with land acquisition and not progressing quickly enough with the development of public services to satisfy the supervisors' voting constituents. In a resolution introduced in April 1919, Eugene Warnimont pointed out the absence of bathing facilities in county parks. Since the water in the Milwaukee River was warmer than Lake Michigan, the demand to provide additional swimming facilities was significant. Blatz Beach (now Kletzsch Park) became a favorite swimming spot.

In 1919, the county board asked the park commission to take on the additional responsibility of developing an airport for Milwaukee County. The site selected was the Zimmerman Farm in Wauwatosa that was recently purchased for the development of Currie Park. By 1925, aviation needs had advanced beyond the capacity of the original landing field, and the commission then played a major role in selecting and purchasing Hamilton Field, the present site of Mitchell International Airport.

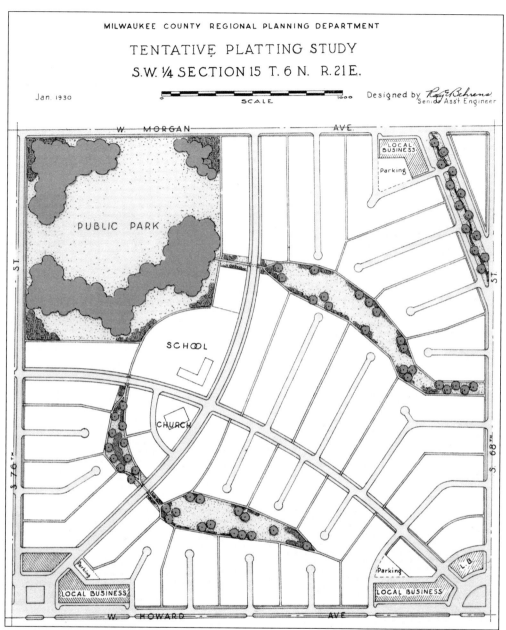

TENTATIVE PLATTING STUDY

S.W. ¼ SECTION 15 T. 6 N. R. 21 E.

Jan. 1930

SCALE

Designed by *Ray E. Behrens*
Senior Asst Engineer

W. MORGAN AVE.

LOCAL BUSINESS

Parking

PUBLIC PARK

SCHOOL

CHURCH

Parking

LOCAL BUSINESS

L B

LOCAL BUSINESS

Parking

W. HOWARD AVE.

Another major development during the 1920s was the creation of the regional planning department under jurisdiction of the park commission. This was the fulfillment of another of Charles Whitnall's long-range goals, made possible by the enactment in 1923 of several pieces of legislation in Madison giving new authority to the commission to control planning and zoned development in the rural areas of Milwaukee. Now the commission had a staff of trained engineers and architects available to provide the technical expertise and assistance necessary to implement their ambitious objectives. Several members of the planning staff, including landscape architect Al Boerner and engineers Ray Behrens and Eugene Howard, were affiliated with the park system for many years and made lasting contributions.

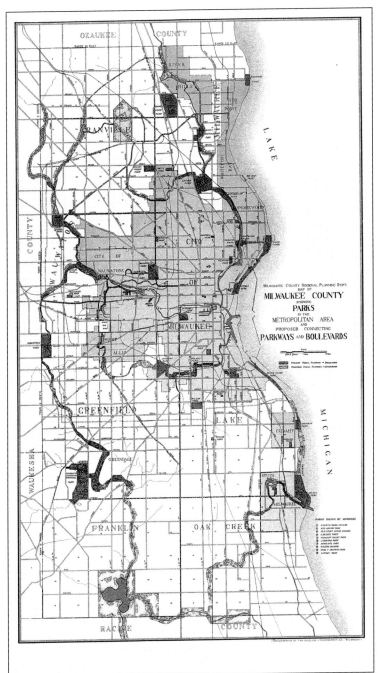

By the summer of 1924, the professionals in the planning department were delivering, on a regular basis, a steady stream of reports, recommendations, and plans for consideration by the commission at its meetings. A glance at a map of the growing park system quickly reveals the operations of two fundamental characteristics of commission policy: the wide geographic dispersion of the parkland and the selection of sites along the county's waterways. By 1930, the park commission had 16 parks under its jurisdiction well distributed throughout the county and offered a wide range of natural and recreational activities.

City of Milwaukee and Milwaukee County park officials are pictured here at a banquet that was held before park consolidation. From left to right are (seated) C. Hauserman; W. F. Borges; A. P. Kletzsch; J. J. Handley; L. J. Timmerman; C. R. Dineen; J. C. Dretzka; G. J. Herrmann; M. P. Kufalk; C. B. Whitnall; and N. Greene; (standing) W. F. Cavanaugh; G. Hansen; W. Grobschmidt; A. J. King; and E. A. Howard. Parks transferred to Milwaukee County included Atkinson Triangle, Bradford Beach, Caesar's Pool, Cathedral Square, Clarke Square, Doctor's Park, Prospect Triangle, Fourth Ward Square, Franklin Nursery, Franklin Triangle, Garden Homes Square, Garfield Park, Gilman Triangle, Gordon Park, Highland Park, Humboldt Park, Jackson Park, Juneau Park, Kern Park, part of the Kinnickinnic Parkway, Kosciuszko Park, Lake Park, Lincoln Park, Lincoln Memorial Drive, Lindbergh Park, McKinley Park, Mitchell Park, Morgan Triangle, Pleasant Valley Park, Pulaski Park (Milwaukee), Riverside Park, Sherman Park, Smith Park, South Shore Park, Walker Square, Washington Park, and Wilson Park. In all, 1,498 acres of park and boulevard at 37 locations were involved. The consolidation movement also saw the following parks transferred to county ownership by other municipalities: Sheridan Park by the City of Cudahy in 1931; Holler Park by the Town of Lake in 1936; Hoyt Park by the City of Wauwatosa in 1937; Pulaski Park (Cudahy) by the City of Cudahy in 1937; and Rawson Park by the City of South Milwaukee in 1937. A total of 42 parks were acquired from other municipalities by the Milwaukee County Park Commission.

Four

THE DEPRESSION AND
THE NEW DEAL

The county park system had grown to impressive proportions by 1930. Two decades after its initial land acquisition, the county parks contained 2,173 acres through purchases totaling $1,384,330. In contrast, the city park board had jurisdiction over 823 acres costing a total of $2,039,621 after its first 20 years of operation.

The wisdom and foresight of this expansion became apparent during the Depression of the 1930s. Money for substantial land acquisition was then nonexistent. Instead, great quantities of funding became available as part of government relief programs set up as part of Pres. Franklin Roosevelt's New Deal program. With the large amounts of relief labor available during the 11-year period from 1931 through 1941, the accomplishments far exceeded those of any other period of equal length in park history. Most of that progress was due to the fact that plans were ready for new developments and improvements when the federal relief labor was made available, practically without notice.

Another result of the financial difficulties of the Depression would be the merging of the county and city park systems. Both the city and the county park systems had operated in tandem until the late 1930s. The Depression had a disastrous effect on city finances. With minimal funding available to the parks, only ordinary maintenance could be carried on. Even when the federal work relief projects were started, the park board could not take full advantage of them, as it did not have funds for the required contribution of materials that the county had.

In an effort to make cutbacks, there was a movement from various civic organizations to merge similar governmental functions. Both the city and the county formed committees to study the possibilities. These committees met separately and jointly over a 10-month period and produced a report that recommended the merging of the city and county park systems. A referendum was included in the regular municipal election of April 7, 1936, to let the citizens of Milwaukee decide the outcome of the city park system for themselves. The referendum passed, and on December 31, 1936, city parks were transferred to Milwaukee County.

In the early part of 1931, as the Depression wore on, it was apparent that some type of relief program would be necessary to bolster the morale of the unemployed. Private industry was unable to support this type of undertaking, making it necessary for municipalities, and later the federal government, to underwrite the expenditures. The first projects were supported under Milwaukee County's Department of Outdoor Relief (DOR). The programs started with four eight-hour workdays per week with a pay rate of 50¢ per hour.

The first of the projects sponsored by the federal government was the Civil Works Administration (CWA), which was inaugurated on November 20, 1933. With less than 48 hours notice, the park commission put approximately 4,000 men to work in the various parks. Practically all of the money appropriated for the CWA was used for personnel services, with very little being expended for materials, as is indicated by the types of projects completed. Many miles of trails and walks were constructed. Primary electric distribution systems were installed in seven of the largest parks and golf courses. Overhead telephone wires with the necessary supporting poles were removed from nine parks with the installation of underground facilities. Sprinkler systems were installed in many of the larger parks. Many thousands of feet of sewers were installed as subdrainage in picnic areas and under baseball diamonds.

Parks were cleaned and athletic fields graded to assist in general maintenance. Underbrush was thinned in wooded areas, and trimming improved the appearance of the trees and shrubs in the parks. Lagoons were created in several parks, and much of the digging was accomplished with the use of hand tools, including the ones seen here at Jacobus and Estabrook Parks.

In Whitnall Park (at the time known as Hales Corners Park), the basic grading for an 18-hole golf course was completed in preparation for spring seeding. In the same park, the crews graded one mile of road 36 feet wide. The CWA, as a program, lasted only eight months, but the accomplishments are comparable to those resulting from programs that followed and lasted much longer.

The CWA program provided the men in the field with warm meals at noon. The park commission operated from 7 to 10 field kitchens, each of which was capable of feeding from 1,000 to 1,500 men. Men from the crews were assigned the job of cooking the daily ration of stew and coffee. The palatability of the meal varied with the ability of the cook.

The Works Progress Administration (WPA) ran from 1935 until 1941 and contributed to the development of practically every park in the system. Six reinforced concrete swimming pools were constructed, complete with filtration plants and bathhouses. The pool at Silver Spring Park (now McGovern Park) was built by the CWA. The WPA built the new bathhouse.

In Brown Deer Park the lagoon was enlarged during the WPA program, and a pavilion of English design utilizing stone and timber was constructed in the side of a hill overlooking the lagoon. A stone-faced arch bridge was built with an opening large enough for skaters and boaters to pass through.

A large outdoor swimming pool was constructed at Greenfield Park by the WPA to serve the western part of the county. The water supply was obtained from a deep well, pumped into small lagoons, or warming basins, where it was "tempered by the atmosphere," and then chemically treated before entering the pool.

The overflow from the Greenfield Park pool supplied the lagoon. In addition to constructing the concrete pool, two warming basins were excavated and graded, stone rills and spillways were constructed, walks around the warming basins were graded, and the area was landscaped.

In 1936, Wauwatosa transferred the 24.7 acres that made up Hoyt Park to the park commission with the condition that a new pool be constructed. The pool in this picture was dug out of an old bed of the Menomonee River and was filled by the fire department pumper.

Later in 1936, the regional planning department prepared plans for the new pool and bathhouse that was then constructed by the WPA. The new facility opened in 1939. The pool had a capacity of one million gallons.

The temporary Grant Park bathhouse at the foot of the Lake Michigan bluff was replaced by the WPA with a permanent building of Colonial design, complete with open-air dressing yards that sat on a raised stone terrace overlooking the beach and lake.

The furniture on the terrace was also designed and built by skilled craftsmen who worked under the federal programs. The 1935 park superintendent's report stated that "One of the most appreciated and talked about places was the bathhouse platform, with its six bright colored tables and umbrellas, which met the fancy of all who came to the beach."

In Whitnall Park, the administration building for the botanical garden was completed and a new golf clubhouse was erected. The buildings were designed by architect George Spinti and constructed by WPA workers using "buttered fieldstone." The building interiors were further decorated with hand-carved woodwork and furnishings crafted by WPA artisans.

This photograph was taken while commissioners and staff from the regional planning department met on site to discuss the appropriate location for Hales Corners (now Whitnall Park) Golf Course clubhouse. Included in the picture are Charles Whitnall (third from the left), who the park would be named for, and Alfred Boerner (far right), who the botanical gardens in the park would be named for.

Another effort taken on by the WPA was the construction of service buildings in Jacobus, Jackson, and Whitnall parks. Depicted here is the Jackson Park service building under construction and after its completion in 1941.

One of the later WPA projects was the construction of the Kosciuszko pool and bathhouse. As one of the parks transferred from the city in 1937, the county set out to update the facilities. Plans for the project were completed in 1939, and approval for funding by the federal government soon followed. Construction for the pool began in 1941. The bathhouse was not completed until 1943.

Another park transferred through the consolidation of the city and county parks was Lapham pool (now Carver Park). The pool and bathhouse were built on the then 1.6-acre site and opened to the public on June 20, 1940. The managing editor of the *Milwaukee Observer*, Charles P. Howard Jr., organized a swim meet at the pool in the summer of 1940 (above). Some of the participants and lifeguards are shown below.

An unusual WPA project involved the relocation of the Kilbourntown house to Estabrook Park. The Greek Revival home was built by pioneer carpenter and master builder Benjamin Church for his family in the early settlement of Kilbourntown near North Fourth and Court Streets. The building was rescued from demolition and moved in four pieces and restored by the WPA in 1938.

The WPA operated a quarry in Currie Park during the entire six-year period from 1935 to 1941. The arrangement was such that the park commission furnished the stone and equipment and the WPA supplied the supervision and labor.

The stone, a rather soft limestone, was used for benches, statuary, copings, and stone slabs for walks and steps that still adorn many of the parks today. This beautiful flagpole base was sculpted and installed in Jacobus Park.

Statues were located in various parks. Artist George Adams Dietrich, a teacher at the Layton School of Art, is shown here with one of his sculptures. Below is a piece he created for the Boerner Botanical Gardens. The statue is located on the edge of a reflecting pool in the perennial borders. Models for the sculpture included Dietrich's wife and Alfred Boerner's son.

The Emergency Conservation Work Act (ECW), better known as the Civilian Conservation Corps (CCC), was in place from 1933 to 1938. With this program, Pres. Franklin D. Roosevelt intended to recruit thousands of unemployed young men and enlist them in a peacetime army "to battle erosion and destruction of the nation's natural resources." On July 1, 1933, camps were established at Sheridan Park, Whitnall Park, and the Honey Creek Parkway.

Young recruits enlisted for a period of six months and received $30 per month. Of that sum, $25 was returned to the recruit's family. After the first enrollment period, those interested could enroll for an additional six months until a total of two years was served. In 1937, the maximum amount of allowable time was reduced to 18 months and the deduction for family allowance was reduced to $22.50.

94

The early work of the CCC was confined chiefly to the parkways. Four camps, including Estabrook, Whitnall, and two at Honey Creek, were in operation between 1933 and 1938. While in camp, all personnel were under the supervision of army officers, but on-the-job supervision was furnished by foremen who were experienced in the various types of construction work involved. Meals were taken at the mess hall on site.

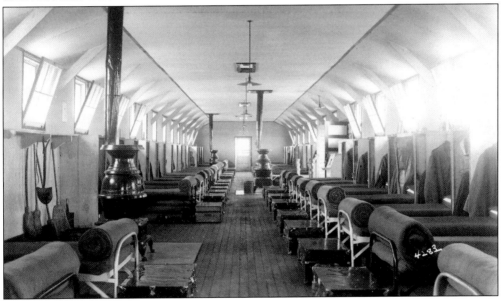

Jerome Dretzka, who served 43 years on the park commission (from 1920 to 1963) acted as procurement officer of the CCC program for all of Wisconsin and upper Michigan. It was his duty to authorize and supervise the purchase of all materials, supplies, and services required by the projects.

Construction on the Honey Creek Parkway was started in late 1932 under the CWA program and continued by the CCC in 1933. The creek and river were relocated in some places. To halt excessive erosion, check dams were installed and retaining walls were built at locations where there were sharp turns.

Six reinforced concrete bridges were constructed along the Honey Creek Parkway, all of which were faced with stone from the Currie Park quarry, including the Ludington Bridge, the Wellauer Bridge, the Gault Bridge, and the Kavanaugh Bridge shown above. A pedestrian bridge was constructed on the Menomonee River Parkway leading into Hoyt Park (below).

One of the largest CCC projects, reported to have involved the services of almost 2,000 men and many pieces of equipment, was located in Lincoln and Estabrook Parks. The Milwaukee River made a complete S-turn in that area, which caused ice jams and floods every spring. After extensive studies by the Milwaukee city engineer's office in collaboration with the regional planning department, it was decided that by straightening the river—which involved the removal of a 6,000-foot-by-200-foot rock ledge in the bottom of the Milwaukee River—future flood damage could be avoided. Workers drilled and blasted the rock and moved it in carts.

The enormous quantity of excavated limestone was then crushed on site (in Estabrook Park) and distributed to various construction projects in the county and used to construct drives, walks, "parking stations," and tennis courts.

A control dam was constructed across the river about a quarter mile east of the Port Washington Bridge. It was to create a lake that would be an attractive feature and prevent seasonal fluctuations of water levels. This dam was composed of two sections separated by a small island. One section was a rock-faced spillway. On the other side of the island were the gates, which were equipped with electrical heating units so that they could be loosened and raised during the winter if necessary.

In Whitnall Park a series of lagoons, roads, and bridges were constructed throughout the 640-acre park by the CCC workers. Whitnall was the only camp operating continuously for the entire six years of the CCC program. One of the remaining tarpaper structures from the camp at Whitnall Park was restored and is still being used by the botanical gardens.

The botanical gardens at Whitnall Park received a jump start with CCC labor constructing most of the walls, walks, and structures in the 50-acre facility. Depicted here is what became a nationally acclaimed rose garden.

A fifth CCC camp was established at Sheridan Park for the purpose of constructing concrete piers or jetties extending into the lake. The problem of holding sand on the beach to reduce the erosion of the steep banks prompted the creation of this project. Materials were brought to the top of the bluff and sent down a chute. Cement was mixed with sand and water on site to create the jetty sections.

A crane placed in the shallow water of Lake Michigan was used to lift the sections while they were lowered and guided into place by the CCC workers. The completion of 11 jetties resulted in the rebuilding of the beach in a short period of time. Similar work was done in Grant Park where the extremely high banks were also in danger of being washed away.

1965

A sixth CCC camp was established at Kletzsch Park, a 118.9-acre park adjacent to the Milwaukee River in Glendale. The crew did some landscape work, but its major project was the replacement of the old crib-type dam, which had been badly damaged and partially demolished by recurring floods.

The new dam was built of reinforced concrete and had, according to a regional planning department report, "a serpentine design to lengthen the crest, thus providing increased capacity without widening the river." A fish ladder was built into the face of the dam.

The dam was faced with limestone to give it the appearance of natural rock. Its design was based on a model constructed by the regional planning department with an appearance similar to rock outcroppings found in rivers north of the county limits.

The shelter in Kletzsch Park was also constructed with relief labor. The 1933–1936 Quadrennial Report of the Milwaukee County Park Commission states that "a new park pavilion, embodying Swiss architectural features was built at the top of the bluff overlooking the Milwaukee River."

Big Bay Park, located along the Lake Michigan shoreline in Whitefish Bay, benefited from shore protection and lannon stone stairs and pathways that provided access down to the beach. They were constructed in 1940 using WPA labor.

This magnificent pavilion was built with relief labor in South Shore Park in 1933. It replaced an earlier bathhouse built in 1912. The park is located on the shore of Lake Michigan in the Bay View neighborhood of Milwaukee.

Thousands of trees were planted using relief labor during the Depression. Trees that were in the way of construction projects were not cut down. Workers excavated around the root ball, and the trees were moved to a new location.

The National Youth Administration (NYA) became active in the park program in 1935 and ran until 1937. They cultivated shrub beds and newly planted trees, mowed lawns, raked leaves, weeded and watered, cleaned up the parks and buildings, worked in the nursery and gardens at Whitnall Park, helped with some of the planting in the parks and parkways, and erected fireplaces for picnic areas.

A large NYA crew was kept at the service department, making benches, picnic tables, and boats; painting; making signs; dismantling obsolete buildings; and helping with the repair and maintenance of equipment. Some of the workers who had clerical training assisted with records and carried on routine office tasks. In many of the jobs, individuals worked as assistants to regular park employees, affording them the opportunity to learn many of the various phases of park operation. They were assigned in groups, chiefly to general maintenance work and in several of the larger parks. The pay rate was approximately 35¢ per hour, and 60 hours of work was allowed each month.

Here the NYA workers proudly display their handiwork at the park sign shop. The increase in demand for labor brought about by improved economic conditions made it possible to place practically all of the boys in private industry, so the project was discontinued in the parks in 1937.

Five

THE POSTWAR BOOM

With the onset of World War II in Europe and the start of a preparedness program in the United States, employment gradually returned to industry and the American economy was rejuvenated. The federal programs were gradually phased out. Following the attack on Pearl Harbor, the park commission halted any new projects in the parks. During the war and for several years after, only necessary maintenance was done. During this same period, the importance of parks to the community expanded. Long vacation trips for families were impossible not only due to shortages of tires, cars, and gasoline, but also due to the long hours and accelerated schedule in industry that allowed no break in production schedules. A greater emphasis was placed on providing recreation and entertainment in the smaller neighborhood parks.

During the war, park employees volunteered and took part in civilian defense programs. Ninety acres of parkland were made available for victory gardens. The park commission cooperated with the United Service Organizations (USO) by issuing free tickets for the various activities in the parks that included programs at the music temple, permits for golf, and tickets for boating, swimming, and tennis for the benefit of servicemen training at Great Lakes and other nearby installations. Fifty-two park commission employees served in the armed services.

Large numbers of workers migrated to Milwaukee during the war to take jobs in the defense industry. Many settled here with their families. Few homes had been built during the war years due to a shortage of materials. At the conclusion of the war, servicemen returned home to a critical housing shortage. Milwaukee County, other communities, and the State of Wisconsin recognized this condition and action was taken. The city and the county mutually agreed on a joint approach to the problem, with the city assuming responsibility for a permanent housing program and the county taking responsibility for temporary housing to meet immediate needs.

In the latter part of 1946, the state legislature enacted measures empowering Milwaukee County to enter the field of public housing. This effort was known as the Veteran's Housing Program and was given to the park commission as the agency best equipped to handle land acquisition and site development.

Another postwar effort for the park commission included a vast public works program that included the development of a baseball stadium, the relocation of the zoo, the construction of a new conservatory at Mitchell Park, the war memorial and art center, development at the lakefront including McKinley Marina, and numerous senior and community and recreation centers.

To meet the immediate housing need, it was decided to place trailers in parks that operated swimming pools, as those parks had toilet and shower facilities in the bathhouses that could be used by the residents. This picture was taken at Kosciuszko Park with the statue of Gen. Thaddeus Kosciuszko as a backdrop.

On December 26, 1946, orders for 407 trailers were placed. Ninety days later, they were all occupied. Also purchased and placed in the parks were 200 prefabricated structures known as Goodyear Wing Foot Homes.

Another type of prefabricated home, manufactured by Haarnischfeger Corporation, was used in large numbers on a site at Wilson Park. The program extended into the mid-1950s, during which time over 900 trailer homes and nearly 765 prefabricated houses provided accommodations for 5,000 families. Eleven long-term housing sites were developed—five for trailer use and the balance for the prefabricated structures.

By 1954, the housing situation had returned to normal, and the park commission recommended that use of trailers and Goodyear Wing Foot Homes units be discontinued. The county board approved, and that phase of the program was terminated on July 1, 1955. The prefabricated houses at the Wilson Park site shown here continued in use for several years longer.

In December 1950, George Hansen, who had been parks superintendent for nearly 25 years, passed away. From the perspective of more than three decades of watching the system grow, Jerome Dretzka recommended the creation of a new administrative structure for the park system headed by a general manager. This new office would be responsible for all administrative duties, including many that he had been performing for years in his dual role as executive secretary and commission member. Alfred L. Boerner, depicted here, was the first person selected to fill the new general manager's post in 1952. Boerner, a longtime landscape architect on the commission's regional planning staff, held the position for only a short three-year period before his death in 1955. The Boerner Botanical Gardens in Whitnall Park were named in his honor.

Boerner's replacement, appointed in early 1956, was Howard Gregg, another veteran member of the staff who had started as a landscape architect in the regional planning department in 1941. Gregg served as general manager for 17 years and retired in 1972. During this time, he presided over a remarkable period of growth, where nearly 5,000 acres were added to the system, new facilities such as the zoo were opened, and programs and services greatly increased.

Another phase of the county's postwar public works program, which became the responsibility of the park commission, was to implement the construction of a community sports stadium. This was regarded as a long-standing need for Milwaukee. Professional baseball was to be the principal beneficiary of the proposed facility. From 1943 to 1945, the local team, the Brewers, had won the American Association championships while performing at Borchert Field, the ancient and rickety ballpark located on the north side. The new stadium opened in 1953.

Although the stadium had been promoted with the hope of someday attracting Major League Baseball to Milwaukee, most Milwaukeeans expected that its tenants for the opening of the 1953 season would be the American Association Brewers, a farm club of the Boston Braves. However, in March 1853, the Boston Braves shattered a half century of fixed major-league geography when they obtained national-league approval to shift the Boston franchise to Milwaukee. The 1953 Milwaukee Braves are posing here at the beginning of the glorious Braves era at County Stadium.

Among the major park commission projects was the establishment of a new zoo. The Washington Park site was considered too small for desired expansion or for substantial remodeling along the lines of modern zoo design that emphasized the use of natural habitat settings. Beginning in 1947, the county began acquisition of land for a new zoo in the area south of Bluemound Road and east of Highway 100 in Wauwatosa. The basic purchases of more than 175 acres were completed in 1964. The new site was almost eight times larger than the Washington Park site.

The design of its facilities emphasized the exhibition of animals and other specimens in their natural settings, according to, where possible, continental groupings. Glass partitions on the inside and hidden moats in open areas virtually eliminated the use of bars. Construction of the first building, the monkey house, began in 1958, and other structures were added at regular intervals so that the Washington Park facility was vacated in 1963.

Samson the gorilla is seen here as a new arrival in 1950 with zoo director George Speidel. Both became longtime fixtures in the zoo. Speidel served as zoo director from 1947 until 1978. He received his training at the Brookfield Zoo from Edward Bean, the first director of the Washington Park Zoo. Speidel is credited with being the driving force behind the building and development of the Milwaukee County Zoo throughout the 1950s and 1960s. Samson the gorilla died of a heart attack at the age of 32 on November 28, 1982. Samson was, perhaps, the most famous animal in the history of the Milwaukee County Zoo. In 1980, the administration of the zoo was separated from the park system and turned over to a special board of the zoological society.

Mitchell Park was historically the site of the conservatory in the old city park system. When a decision was made to replace the old conservatory with a modern structure, the site remained the same. Architect Donald L. Grieb was commissioned to design the new structure.

Grieb suggested a beehive design using three domelike structures with each housing different plant communities. Since this was a new design concept, new construction methods were engineered. A concrete frame was precast on site. A "skin layer" of aluminum tubing and reinforced glass was placed over a temporary structure until it was self-supporting. Finally, the three-ton, 37-foot-diameter caps were placed on each 85-foot-high dome.

The first of the domes was opened in December 1964 with a Christmas display. The Tropical Dome, highlighted by its 25-foot waterfall, was completed by January 1966, and the Arid Dome (shown here) was opened to the public in October 1967.

The domes were officially dedicated in 1965 with first lady Claudia Alta "Lady Bird" Johnson presiding over the ceremonies. She is shown here touring the facility with longtime park landscape architect Lee Egelhoff (on her right) and a cadre of press and Secret Service agents.

In the closing years of World War II, community interest was expressed for the construction of a suitable memorial to the men and women from Milwaukee County who served in the armed forces. Construction of the war memorial began in 1955. Designed by architect Eero Saarinen, the building would also provide facilities for the Milwaukee Art Center (later named the Milwaukee Art Museum).

Beginning in 1959, the park commission again set out with an ambitious plan to develop a public marina. The initial development included some 1,250 feet of sheet pile bulkhead, thousands of yards of fill, and underground utilities at a cost of half a million dollars. An eight-lane launch ramp was part of this initial phase.

In late spring of 1963, work was started on the installation of 4,200 linear feet of steel bulkhead, extending from the existing shoreline at the south end of the Juneau Park lagoon out into Lake Michigan to a point 500 feet from the federal government breakwater.

This bulkhead defined the limits of a 70-acre landfill project that created a protected harbor for the McKinley Marina. The landfill, including the area that was known as the Juneau lagoon, became today's Veterans Park.

By the time of its completion in 1979, the marina project included the reclamation of more than 70 acres through a massive landfill operation and the creation of more than 650 anchoring slips for sailing enthusiasts.

Facilities for senior citizens groups and more sophisticated buildings offering a wide range of recreational programs for all ages became an important part of the park system in the 1960s and 1970s. At Washington Park in 1968, the first of a half-dozen new, modern senior centers was dedicated.

The senior centers featured a myriad of recreational opportunities. The center courtyard of the Washington Park Senior Center featured a scent garden in raised planting beds. A group of visually impaired seniors are shown here enjoying the facility.

The Dr. Martin Luther King Jr. Community Center reflects still another important trend in park development during the 1960s and 1970s; namely, an effort to increase a park presence in the central city and downtown area of Milwaukee. Land for King Park was acquired by the park commission in 1971 from the city redevelopment authority, and federal funding was instrumental in the development of the site and construction of the community center building.

Clifford R. Pitts served as the first director of the community center. In the June 6, 1976, grand opening program, Pitts was quoted as saying, "I shall do my utmost to incorporate into every activity programmed in the Community Center and Park the philosophy of the late Dr. Martin Luther King, Jr., that all men and women, boys and girls—regardless of race, creed, color, or national origin—can work and play together in harmony with love being the catalytic agent."

The Dr. Martin Luther King Jr. Community Center was built with 43,000 square feet of space and was the only building in the parks with a full-scale gymnasium. It also was the only park with special facilities for boxing instruction. Instruction courses were held for training of boxing teams for Golden Gloves competitions. "Taking it outdoors" had a different meaning at the community center, where two young men show off their boxing skills.

Ice-skating became a year-round activity with the opening of the Wilson Park Recreation Center on January 24, 1970. Skating took many forms at the facility, including speed skating and special sessions for families and groups. The Milwaukee Admirals hockey team played its games at the rink for many years.

An Olympic-size pool opened in 1971 adjacent to the ice facility in Wilson Park and hosted five competitive swim meets that first season. Attendance for public swimming, lessons, and other aquatic events topped 114,000 that year.

124

The recreation division was an important component of the park operations. By 1970, parks programs included golf and tennis tournaments; swim meets; senior and youth dances; golf, tennis, and archery instruction; basketball, softball, soccer, and football leagues; skate capades; overnight camping; a fishing rodeo; skating meets; and table tennis tournaments, just to name a few. In the above photograph, tennis star Arthur Ashe is featured at a tennis clinic at Washington Park in 1968. In the photograph below, a bait-casting clinic is held outside the Lincoln Park's Blatz Pavilion in June 1963.

Winter sports are an important part of the long Wisconsin winters. The 1958–1959 season reported ice-skating at 54 locations, including 20 lagoons, 31 rinks, and three rivers. Figure skating instructions were held at nine park locations. Sledding was also a favorite winter activity in many of the parks. During the 1959 season, the parks had toboggan slides at four parks—Jackson, Riverside, Whitnall, and the one shown in this 1968 photograph at Brown Deer Park.

On May 11, 1975, Milwaukee County Parks dedicated its newly expanded bike trail system called the Milwaukee 76 as part of Milwaukee Area Bike Week. The name was chosen not only to commemorate the bicentennial of the American Revolution, but also to reflect that the trail was now 76 miles long. A biker consults the trail map along the trail at Bay View Park.

DISCOVER THOUSANDS OF LOCAL HISTORY BOOKS FEATURING MILLIONS OF VINTAGE IMAGES

Arcadia Publishing, the leading local history publisher in the United States, is committed to making history accessible and meaningful through publishing books that celebrate and preserve the heritage of America's people and places.

Find more books like this at
www.arcadiapublishing.com

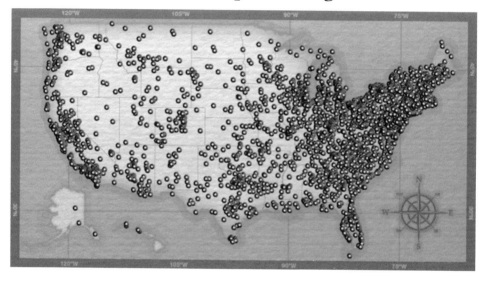

Search for your hometown history, your old stomping grounds, and even your favorite sports team.